THE
WINGS
OF
ADVERSITY

THE WINGS OF ADVERSITY

VANESSA CARAVEO

Published in Los Fresnos, TX, U.S.A.

ISBN: 978-1-7333798-4-7 (Paperback)

Library of Congress Control Number: 2020900966

Ordering Information:
For details, contact the publisher at the address below.

Vanessa Caraveo
P.O. Box 93
Los Fresnos, TX, 78566

Printed in the United States of America

First Edition

First Printing, 2020

This collection of poems is dedicated to you. You're stronger than you know. You'll always find light at the end of every tunnel.

TABLE OF CONTENTS

ILLNESS AND DISABILITY

CULTURAL ADVERSITY

HEROES OF ADVERSITY

EMPOWERMENT THROUGH ADVERSITY

ILLNESS AND DISABILITY

Your illness does not define you. Your strength and courage does.

—Unknown

AN AWAITED BALANCE

The wind blows my curtains in fury,
challenging me as it does every night,
but it gets disappointing when I just stare,
without making an effort to heed its call.
It's another night's call;
only this time, it's in a new way
perhaps, it has lost its strength,
or its fury has been quenched
because it blows calm,
making me listen to its voice for the first time.
I never thought nature could understand a human;
I once thought I would never be understood.
I turn to face my open windows,
enjoying the gentle sweep of the wind.
I stretch my arms to hold this feeling
since my feet cannot take me to my window.
The first time in a long time
something or someone truly cared for my feelings.
It didn't force me to move as fast as it does;
rather, it slowed its pace to bring me along.

A DREAM

The light shines into the room,
adding colors to the gloomy atmosphere.
The faint whispers of a machine can be heard
at the extreme end of the room, beeping, vibrating.

A man cradles the body of a woman to himself,
lost to the fear that comes with the sounds.
Her eyes are closed and her body is limp.
She is with him, but her mind is far away, it seems.

Perhaps she will wake someday or never from this coma,
and tell him tales of her dreams while she slept.
They funnel nutrients into her, day in, day out,
hoping in a few days, she will be up and about.

That hope has lasted a few months now, and slowly,
the lights fizzle out of his eyes and his prayers.
But like a devoted mother,
he watches over her like a mother hen
never missing any sound
or movement he hopes she makes.

His heart is heavy with doubts and fears of the ugly truth,
and he wishes she doesn't cross to the underworld
without a proper 'bye,
without a chance to gaze upon her smile.

He reads her favorite stories to her
and feels a finger move;
once, twice and again.
The longest he has had from her in a long time.
He cries in joy,
for all hope is not lost.

FLORENTINA

I am close to the hay of the sickbay,
Flopping lifelessly on the floor is my trademark.
I don't play with the swing, a pastime for lasses of my age.
I can't eat what others crunch,
Nor punch bullies with life in my hand.

I once asked Dad why he christened me Florentina.
He said, "Beautiful lasses bear beautiful names."
I wasn't convinced.
Phoebe calls me an imp.
She said, "I am a wilted flower which causes trouble."
Wilted doesn't seem right, but I know I am fragile.

Perhaps Dad called me Florentina for I am his fragile egg,
Or because I need gentle tendering, unlike most lasses.
With a bent back and a pair of crouched knees,
He tends his wilted flower day and night.

The wilted flower now blooms in a merchant's vase.

I became a rose;
One that scents
Without fainting.

I became a rose;
With Dad as the horticulturist
And Mom as the smiling sun.

HANDS OF A MILLION EMOTIONS

DUM-DUM-DUM...
The beating drums rhythmically rolled in.
It could be heard from miles away.
I closed my eyes and moved my feet,
slowly following the drum beats.
It became faster at each passing minute
until I stood to dance with the beats.

DO-RE-MI
The pianist picked a beautiful note
as she composed a song with her hands.
My hands glided to press the imaginable keys
as the bliss of the music seeped into my soul.

Music, a companion in the good and hard times,
my love for it never faltered,
but I could feel something missing,
a lack that chained my feelings up within me.

THE VOICE
I can play the guitar with my eyes closed.
I know every string by heart,
but I cannot sing along
since an illness took my voice.
That is my missing note.
I can only sing with my hands and heart,
but happiness lives on my face and within my soul.

A HEIGHT NOT FRIGHT

We may all be born of a woman,
but do not grow at the same pace;
others may be shorter than most,
and others taller than most.

Like others, he was born of a woman,
but he developed a tree's leg.
His friends were frightened to see him,
for he stood three feet ahead of others.
Like a bird, he stood at a vantage point over others
while they were forced to marvel at his legs.

It was a good view at first,
until he got uncomfortable with his height.
He could be seen from a far distance
as he dangled through the crowd with ease.

I am taller than the height of men,
this I know very well.
But it is just a height not meant for fright,
I am a man like you.
I am living with it and not living like you.
I live with the stares of many anytime I am outside.
It bothers me no longer;
if only they knew;
it is just some height,
and I'm not a fright to gaze upon.

A CHOICE OF THE MIND

Think deep but not too deep;
  Unanswered questions sing deep in my heart;
    My eyes are sunken from being in my world
        Since no one understands the pressure I feel within.

I wield my pen in the curve of my heart,
Bent but pointing at one direction.
Some call me crazy for soliloquizing,
If only they could understand the weakness of my mind.

I have been counseled to control my thoughts.
  I have been told I possess the power to direct my mind.
    But I struggle like a goose searching for its mother
        Whenever I try to understand myself.

I lost my thoughts when I lost my mother;
It was a shock like no other.
I tried to move on from the trauma,
But how does one forget a loved one?

To find a balance is still an option,
One I am uncertain of its bearing.
For now, let them frown at my choice
Till I am healed from my mind,
But I may remain a slave to my trauma
Until death comes for me.

But now that I am alive, I won't budge to my fears.
I must make a choice to make my mind right again.

UNSTEADY VOICE

I was hungry and starved,
battered by the little options I had in life.
My hunger was not for food or for water;
I was thirsty for options, to choose my course in life.
I was born with a stutter,
making my words slow and my speech longer.
I envied those with a smooth tongue,
for they spoke with the flow of their emotions.
There was a dagger in my heart
whenever I had to wait for a second to express my words.
I seemed to lose the weight of my emotions
when held by my stuttering tongue at those times.
I had ideas, but I was a captive to my mouth.
I had wild emotions, but I was told to wait a little longer.
I wanted to sing,
but I couldn't keep the melody in my voice.
My unsteady voice was a burden I carried
until I fell in love with my pen and paper.
And today, I have become a celebrity from writing.
All my emotions and ideas,
I document, without the usual stutter.

MY LIFE

Rrring!!!
It's 6 am
Stop the alarm
Drop the blanket
Walk to the bathroom
Wait for your turn
While your partner washes
Grab your brush
Grab your towel
Take a bath
Dress for work
Rush a bowl of cereal
Flag a bus

Honk!!!
Board one to work
Enjoying the bustling of the day
Then a sudden crash behind a desk
Rushed to the clinic in a panic
After a while
Now wide awake
But too weak to talk
Feeling ashamed
So, a pair of eyes are tightly closed
A familiar voice speaks
"It's okay. No one is here.
Open your eyes."
Feeling relaxed, eyes are opened
But stare toward the door
From the reach of the familiar voice

The voice continues,
"Use your drugs
Do not stress yourself. Worry less.
Let your heart heal.
Take it a step at a time."

Used to this
Nods at all messages
With a heavy eye
And a heavier heart
Lays on a side
Waiting for the day
To live a normal life
With no fainting spells
Despite having a family to cater for
It will be soon
The familiar voice confirmed it

FAITHFUL FATE

I love the hills in the coastal regions.
They sit with pride on their faces.
No matter the size or shape they take,
A hill it is and still would be,
A faithful fate they enjoy without complaints.

Predestined from the womb with a fate,
Chosen without a blink in the eyes.
The years spoke to the silent air
And never asked how I would survive it.
It was a fate already given;
One where I already mastered its art
Without much instruction.

My legs were formed curved, making movements slow.
My neck was slightly bent like a broken headlamp.
I need not explain my predicament
Since it was so faithful to show itself to everyone.
My status chose to share the spotlight with me
Before anyone knew I was the one with the disease.

I am often ignored for being inept at things
Since my body wasn't wired for many activities.
And this fate remained ever faithful
In keeping me at the back of every ride.
But the back gave me a better view of life,
One I may have never seen or cared to notice.
There is beauty in the world.
I am glad I have this seat all to myself.

ETERNAL MEMORIES

My mother's love was more precious than the world to me,
and my mama was the epitome of such rare beauty.
Her world calmed my aching heart.
Her soothing palms caressed my spine,
and called me to a night of blissful sleep.
My mother was like no other; I had just myself and her,
and I was the only one who understood her every action.

Many said she was a beauty in her youth,
but she lost her all before death, even her senses.
They said she didn't even recognize her son
and should be locked up in a psychiatric home.

They didn't know she always took her medicine.
They didn't know she checked on me every night.
They didn't know she sang to me when I was sad.
Come to me my son, she always said,
as her eyes would light up when I returned home.

I smiled and reached for her warm embrace.
She sighed as she drew me into her arms.
I will survive this, my son, she whispered,
*for no sickness can take the beautiful memories
that I have of you from me.*

And with tears in my eyes, I hugged her tightly,
because I knew she'd get better,
even if the world thought otherwise.
For what is a memory loss compared to the love
of a mother and her warm embrace?

LET ME BREATHE

The world is large, but I feel choked.
I am given space, but it's not enough.
The beauty of life is one I love,
And I do not want to lose any moment it gives.
To enjoy life, I am given another breath,
One I lean on in the most uncomfortable times.
I take my second breath with me everywhere;
I ensure it is within my reach at all times.

Not everyone is born with this burden.
Not everyone needs a second breath in life.
There are times I thought of days,
Without taking my companion with me,
But the fear of the unknown convinces me
That I cannot rely on my first breath.

I feel uncomfortable
Under the watchful gaze of friends and family,
Watching my every move and turn.
A burden it indeed is to bear,
But I know they care for me more than anything else.

A relaxed shoulder may cause me a deadly slip,
But a relaxed mind will lead to a stronger breath.
I won't fail to breathe even if I am fragile,
For my breath is a priceless treasure I must guard.

AN AUGUST VISITOR

Your arrival is always unexpected,
Turning the lives of many in disarray.
The lucky ones battle you and overcome;
Sadly, you take some with you without a second glance.

You are not particular about your choice
Since you take both the old and young,
Arriving in different forms
But with almost the same result at the end.

Cancer, how terrible you are.
Many people weep for freedom from you,
But you spread your wings on them, notwithstanding.
You make beautiful hair fall at your feet,
You weaken their strong bones
And cause them to endure the pricks on their flesh.

Some have subdued you.
Your hold is now weakening.
Your stance is now shaking.
You will soon be sent packing to the end of the world.

An August visitor you are,
And your time will come to go
And never return to torment the lives of humankind.

IT'S IN YOU

You are not alone in this.
Those were the words
I spoke to myself when alone.
My eyes were red from sleeplessness,
my arms trembled from my restlessness.
It was not an intentional act,
it just chose to happen without a trigger.
I had a lot to say, but expressions were hard to form.
I could see the impatience in some people's eyes
when I took long to assimilate their ideas.
My tongue was usually trapped
when asked questions I should know.
I wish I could break free from it,
but I was born to live with it.

I grew up an introvert,
always playing with flip-flops around me.
I picked a pace I set for myself
since I understood me
more than any other person.
One day,
I saw a livewire performance on my screen,
and my love for music
sprang like wildfire.
The guitar seemed to understand my every question
and my silent thoughts.
I spoke through the strings
and let my emotions direct my hands.

Many wondered
how an autistic patient
could be so good at music
when they couldn't understand simple gestures.
Many asked how I was able to play
with my eyes closed
when I couldn't read well
with my eyes open.
Many queried
how my music teacher taught me

when I always shied away
from the slightest body contact.
Many wondered
how I was able to sit
for hours to learn to play the guitar
when I had trouble
adapting to new routines.

But I told them,
in the best way that I could,
that autistic patients
also have interests
like every other individual;
they could also learn new skills
if taught with love.

HEAVEN'S CALL

I long
For a home far from here,
A place where there is no grief or pain.

I long
For a home far from here,
Where my feebleness is overlooked.

I long
For a home far from here,
A place where sickness is nonexistent.

I long
For a home far from here,
A place where I am treated like every other person.

I long
For a home far from here,
Where pity is replaced with love by most people.

I heard of a place where it exists,
But it is far from here.
I want that home here on earth.
I want heaven to hear my call.

Heaven, hear my cry:
Bring that paradise I crave
To me on Earth,
And take this sickness away.
I hope you pick my call,
And give me a new life without pain
Because I believe
I will get better.

MY SHADOW

Looking into the past
makes it more complicated than I imagined.
Thoughts about the future
leave marks of uncertainties on my burdened self.

The past was trying to grab
a shadow every hour,
a shadow that left
at the crack of dawn of each passing day.

It is difficult to see one stand
by you in the hardest times.
Even my shadow chooses when to come and go.

There are times
I feel the pointed dagger of pain,
telling me to say the last prayer
before I surrender to its givings.

I laugh hysterically at my shadow
when we are together,
especially when I watch it slip
behind like a guardian angel;
only it cannot be there at all times
when the pain makes me cry out in agony.

I live each day
with the hope of moving through,
believing winning, and not losing,
is what I must get in all of this adversity.

ONE LEG AND A STUMP

A spotlight should be beamed on the street.
Some beings shouldn't be rooted in a ruthless spot.
Instead, they should be routed toward places with light.

Aliya talked about the bleeps she heard
when her distorted soul
bade one of her legs goodbye.
It seemed as if the machine silenced the joy around her.

Life used to be a bed of roses
until the roses revealed the thorns beneath them.
The thorns pricked her with the sweet revelation
of a tough journey
and the beginning of her bloody nightmare.

Her parents succumbed their breaths
to the accident that claimed one of her legs.
The rest of the family tree sold her out,
defying the dead's will because they failed to write a will.

The street became her home;
shacks became her dwelling place.

Today, we met,
and she told me her story.
She had since been learning how to walk
with a crutch without help.
Soon, she will take to the skies
with her dreams and soar high.

NINETY-NINE MIRRORS

Words can hurt when used wrongly.
It can break a person's stance
and then leave him or her lonely.
They hurt more when it shows a truth,
one you try hard to hide from the world.

The rebellious mirror sits proudly on my fattened lap.
It eyed me with disgust on its shiny face.
I think of ways to wipe its smirk off its face,
but it still would be the same with every one I get.

This is the ninety-ninth mirror I have bought,
yet I see no changes in me in them.
It's like they called each other to discuss my plight,
and they enjoy the same satisfaction
they get on my tired face.

I stare at my plump face
and lift my fat stabbed arms.
It keeps growing even when I feed on greens,
a disorder the doctor said was rare.
I eagerly await the solution to my plight,
but I won't hide from people again.
I will enjoy every moment like I am meant to.

OVER HERE

She moved so fast that I almost lost my balance.
She said to follow her movement if I wanted to be free.
Over here, she moved her hands beckoning at me.
I was fast to understand since I read lips well.

Rigid at first, I eased the tension in my shoulders
Until I followed her every movement.

We sat for a while after our daily exercise,
Panting and gasping for air.
My face was flushed from the practice,
And a part of me was glad it was over.

Over here, she said again, pointing to an empty chair.
I nodded and sat in it, ready for another day of learning.
I stretched my left palm toward her,
Awaiting the ministrations.
I felt her fingers on me as she soothed the pain
With a silent message.
I understood the message of each stroke
On the lines of my palms.

Do not give up, she wrote, a smile on her face.
I nodded.
And although my palm was my ears,
My eyes and my mouth,
I will make the best of her message.

SOMEONE IS WATCHING

On a stormy night, there would be drumrolls
from all cardinal points.
Feet would run helter-skelter for shelter.
The streets would be swept clean from the wild wind;
houses built on the sand would whisper in prayers
of not wanting to lose their foundation in the angry storm.

Every day is a storm for me.
I run from no one in particular but everyone.
In the darkest places and on the brightest days,
my mind harbors a pretentious tension in my brain,
releasing sparks of fear in my already shaken body.

ANXIETY! ANXIETY! ANXIETY!
No matter the number of times I call,
she never releases her stronghold on me.
I have lived with her for as long as I could walk.

I have been robbed of my many gifts
because I felt someone was always watching.
The four walls of my room hold no comfort,
since every turn and sound
sends a nervous alert to my mind.
I took a step to look through my windows.
The stars waved at me.
For the first time in forever,
I feel at ease that someone is indeed watching me.

I LIVED

Twenty years ago,
I was born, like every child,
Only I was different
From the other little ones.

A scientific fault was found in my stars
Because I was born
With a defected spine.
The doctors held my parents' hands,
Words failing them as they sought to ease their pain.

Then they turned to me
And cradled me carefully,
And that was how I began my journey.

I was born with spina bifida,
Making me indifferent to some physical pain,
Although my heart throbbed with pain from within.

At first,
I was made a special walking shoe,
One that they said
Would cause some sort of discomfort,
But the illness didn't make me bother
Since I felt little or no pain.

I once bumped my foot on a stone
Just like anyone could have done,
But I only landed myself in the hospital
As if I didn't deserve a normal life, too.

My movement was monitored
By everyone ever since,
For they feared
I might unknowingly inflict harm
On my fragile self
Since I rarely felt
More than a little sensation on my body.

As the years went by,
Many thought I wouldn't survive
Since I spent most of my time
At the hospital, my second home,
Until I was confined to a wheelchair.

But the wheelchair didn't confine my life
Or my dreams of a beautiful existence.
I began learning all the news things
Everyone thought I was incapable of doing by myself
In order to prove everyone wrong
And that I am still human,
Even if I was different.

So, I did normal things
Like every other person.
I loved, I lived and I laughed
And proved everyone wrong.

CULTURAL ADVERSITY

It is not our differences that divide us. It is our inability to recognize, accept, and celebrate those differences.

—Audre Lorde

LET US BEGIN

We cannot remain an outcast forever
because we do not know the ways of our host.

We cannot keep quiet when we want to talk
because we cannot speak a foreign language.

We cannot shy from public gatherings
because we do not know the history behind the meeting.

Now, we may be there, by choice or not,
but we can make a move to live our best lives.
It may be hard accepting a new norm;
it may be challenging learning to speak again;
it may be difficult learning the alphabet again,
but we can give it a try.

Let us begin now;
make the house a home again.
There are consequences to moving to a new place.
If we do not welcome the changes,
we cannot make a new change.

Let us begin now,
not later,
not tomorrow,
or the next day.

Now is the time to make a change.

OUTSIDE

There is a special richness on every coast.
There is a special calm each place holds.
There is a special touch every abode leaves.

There is a special scent
That holds the mind captive in dreams.

There is a special view
That cannot be compared to another.

There is a special song
That sounds sweet in only that language.

Look outside:
The sky is painted in the colors of everyone's heart.
It represents the picture we all want to see,
Making us love what we choose to see alone.

Look outside:
What happens when we all look at the sky?
It becomes painted in different colors,
Although it can form a beautiful picture
If we come together.

Look outside:
There are people everywhere,
Blacks, whites, Hispanics and many more,
Having different heritages and personalities,
But one thing can bring them together
When they look beyond the outside appearance: love.

PROTECT ALL

I am called partial when I protect my own,
but many seem to forget it was caused by us all.

We made obstacles of our adversity,
creating roadblocks on every path we pass.

We shelter those who bear semblance with us.

We shelter those who speak like us.

Even when they do the wrong,
we neglect their wrong.

Many people think like that,
making it hard for us to fit in with each other.
The rigid backs refuse to be flexible
to create an opportunity for a visitor.
Protection is good, but you should reprove the guilty.
Come down from your high horses,
and let us see one another as one.

Our love for our kind is strong,
but there are some who come from another part.
Some find it hard to settle in,
especially when made a stranger in a strange land,
despite the years spent together.
Protect all and not a selected few!

I SHALL SEE MY HOME

Like rhymes
Sang to pupils,
Dad tells me
Stories of our Black roots.

We live abroad
But our first abode
Was in the depths of Africa.

The weather overseas
Didn't change our color.
We are black, full melanin.

We were called apes,
Made to live in bordered houses,
Forced to do menial jobs.

Cops pry into our souls;
We can't be innocent.
Jails should be our home.

Hardcastle called me an ape,
I threw punches at him...
I was being led to jail.

The jail is a cold place,
A place designed with cruelty.
A place fit for apes.

I was jeered at;
Dad lost his high spirit.
Some advice flew in the air:
Call an attorney!

As I laid on the cold floor,
Sounds of flutes filled my head:
A call from my native place.
When shall I see my home?
I open my eyes

And see beyond the walls of this border.
I see the shadow of my home.
I know soon I shall be home again.

ALEJANDRO

My life has always been an interesting one,
for those who understand my ways and accept me.
It's a pity only a few do
because the *others* see me as an outsider.

I have lived outside my home
for as long as time could count,
yet there are no changes in my origins in me.
For the Latino blood runs in me,
which I carry along like a backpack
in every journey I make.

Some mornings, I have my chilaquiles,
much against the angry stares of some colleagues
who see it strange, unlike the famous bacon and eggs.

The stinging remarks burn, but I cover it up
with the satisfaction that I feel within.
There are times I argue over their insensitive remarks,
but it just increases the tension we each feel.

We have worked together for a decade,
but there was always a dark cloud around us.
It was one brought by us,
which can only be cleared by us,
if we erase all differences and come together as one.

THE SCHOOL WALLS

The school is big to accommodate many.
The classes are wide to have enough chairs,
Yet they seem too small at times.
Since there were *classes* in the classes,
A sad realization for some students.

The hallway is filled with students,
But can easily in a second become a place for two *classes,*
The famous and the weirdos.
It is a wonder how racism came to be in some schools
Where segregation is made to rule.
A student's heritage may be his downfall,
Thus making many people hide who they are.
They become embarrassed about sharing their history
From the fear of being kicked aside.

A smile is plastered on their faces,
But their mind is a reminder of their home.
They hold on to it in the quiet room,
Wishing the world would accept them with open arms.
The high school has its turns and expectations,
But home will always be there to welcome all.

THE GATHERING

A meeting of kings and queens
from different parts of the world.
All uniquely dressed,
they richly display their culture for all to understand.
To each representative of their countries,
they flaunt their beautiful clothes
adorned with traditional accessories,
as they each try to outshine the other,
not giving each other a chance
to do better than the other.

I sigh deeply at this,
as they have forgotten the purpose of the gathering.
They are consumed by the pride of their culture,
forgetting the purpose is to unite all.

Who will tell them?
That they need not flaunt at each other.

Who will tell them?
That they are already the best of their kind.

Who will tell them?
That they can bring their differences to make a difference.

Eagles need not announce their presence to other birds,
for their strength can be felt from afar.
But they do not act like friendly eagles at the moment.
Someday they will learn from one another
and identify they fly with the same feather.

AN UNBREAKABLE BOND

She said, 'Je vais revenir.'
I closed my door and smiled at those words.
I have come to slowly understand her ways,
though the journey has been taxing from the start.

I am in love with my French lady,
one whose coyness makes me eager
to learn from her.
But I fear for the unexpected waves of the future,
the joining of two identities as one.

I fear the gap in our communication,
for we speak in different tones.
I fear for an uncertain welcome from her people
who may frown at the alien in their midst.

But our bond can't be broken,
even if we come from two different worlds,
even if our colors differ.

I crave for an unbroken bond with her,
and despite the dissenting heads
gathered to break this bond,
I won't mind pulling her
into my embrace again
because love and understanding
are all we need to save us from
the heartache of breaking this bond.

THE STAR OF HOPE

It
was
my first
winter
since I was
born. In fact, none
of my family had
experienced any. My folks and I
were welcomed by the cold weather.
Unbothered, we stood in awe appreciating
the beautiful buildings we saw. It was nothing like
Africa, our home. The contrast was obvious that we needed no map to point the
differences. We held hands outside the airport, happy we had made it to our
dreamland. But we looked into the sky, searching for the star
that spelled hope; some hope for a better future.
The cold did not warn us ahead of the lonely days. The big house
did not tell us about its wish to be filled with friends.
Like a child who was naïve of his new environment,
we entered this new land living with enthusiasm
and joy. Every day was a new lesson,
more of a lesson on what to do or say. We
struggled to adapt to every new development at work.

We had a few friends	since we were new
and colored,	but we knew the
cold welcome would	fade as time grew.
And when we did	look up this time,
there was a	star in the sky,
blinking	faintly.
Our star	of hope.

THE TRIALS OF MY FAITH

Everywhere my friends and I turn,
we meet blocks and barricades in the form of humans
who believe us the enemy.

Our bearded faces send them scurrying into hiding,
and our hijabs leave them scared out of their wits.
Some spit in our faces and curse us with their eyes.
Others, too scared of what we may do, run for dear life.

We sigh and bow our heads as their whispers trail after us.
We shake our heads and pray for them as they mock us.
Some claim we bombed their brothers to hell.
Others claim we are just nothing but suicide bombers
who believe their reward lies at the gates of Al Jannah
when they meet their maker.

But I tell my friends that we should raise our shoulders
and bow our heads in prayer, even as we wave to them
and wear a beautiful smile on our faces.

Because I know that someday
we will all fall into an embrace,
Muezzins, Fathers, and Buddhists alike,
and no one will gaze upon anyone in fright any longer.

THE FAR END OF THE TABLE

The year is coming to an end.
The road is lighted with beautiful decorations.
Children can be heard practicing the carols,
As they sing joyfully to every tune.

In the comfort of our homes,
A few of my friends planned a day together,
As many would travel for the holiday.
It started on a happy note until it took another turn.

We brought varieties of food,
Leaving choices for us to make.
Dawn brought a special course her family makes.
She was filled with joy for having it shared by others.

Only, no one wanted it.
It was a strange food to all,
And such had a perfect spot,
At the far end of the table.

Her face was crushed at what she saw,
But she pretended it was nothing.
I placed my arm around her shoulders.
It was the silent communication that her sad spirit needed.

We are from different cultures,
But I accepted who she was.
She smiled and nodded
As we took a step many will later use to fall in line.

EVERYWHERE YOU GO

People make up the planet Earth;
without them, it would be empty.
The water would overflow without anyone to use it.
The ground would be dusty,
and the Earth would be silent.

We are spread all over the Earth,
but the wind calls us together.
Our eyes itch to see beyond our horizon,
and our feet lead the eyes to any place they wish to go.

Everywhere you go, we are greeted with a peculiarity.
We meet the same humans but with different creativity.
They are sculptured to fit their society,
creating many humans with their roots in hand.

Everyone holds on to his or her foundation
everywhere they go in life,
but sadly, not all foundations can fit in a picture,
for we are yet to openly shake hands in agreement.

Everywhere you go,
a new event happens,
mostly different from our beliefs and customs.
We stare opened-eyed at them,
and some frown at them.
Yet, it doesn't change their belief
because everywhere you go,
there is something new you see.

A BETTER LAND

Our earth is slowly losing its shelter.
War is tearing through the lands.
The days are slowly fading
From covered light
As our haven has become
A rowdy street.

But times have changed the course
Because a chaotic environment
Can be the birth of danger.
Families meet to make a decision
Since their homes are no longer safe.
Their stomachs growl in hunger,
For parents barely earn enough
To feed their children.

The cry of hunger
Can be seen on their faces,
Thus, causing desperation
In the hearts of men.
The impatient seek deadly options
As a means of survival,
Forgetting the principles
Of patience and perseverance.
A decision must be made soon and fast;
A new home is one we need
But far away
From where we are.

Hands are tied
With little choices to consider.
It hurts
To leave one's birthplace for another,
But life must go on
For everyone, and we must survive.

For how long
Will the suffering continue?
Two meals a day is a luxury,

And a meal is a blessing.
Whereas we can eat plenty
And live well if we leave.
At least
The children deserve a better life.
It is time to pack our bags.

We are set
And ready for the big move,
A move to a greener pasture.
We have little or no choice to make
Since the future of many generations
Depends on it.
We are prepared
For what lies ahead
As long as we have a filled tummy
And assurance of a better life.

We will move
To a better land,
The USA,
A Canaan for everyone,
A place
Where we hope to be accepted.

LOVE AND PEACE

You will walk in peace,
even on the darkest roads,
if love is in your heart
and peace is on your lips.

You will shake hands
with a lot of people,
even when you do not know their heritage,
if love lives in you and you preach peace.

You will learn new skills,
even if the method is different from the familiar,
if you open your heart to change.

You will understand foreign tongues,
even though it may take some time,
if you are curious about knowledge.

You will visit many places,
even if their ways are not like yours,
if you thirst for more company.

You will be accepted as one of them,
even if you are new on the job,
if you want to relate to other people.

You will walk in peace
without glancing over your shoulder in fear,
if you care for other people.

The soil may be different
from what you knew,
yet I know
you'll learn to grow on a new one,
just as many others
have done before you.

There are bridges between every culture,
each built to suit the place they come from.

But we can mend the broken bridges
if we decide to let go of our adversities.

A person's culture
should not be a problem for someone else
because we can fit both together
and create a bigger one.

There is a time for personal glory
and a time to commend one another,
but it can only be done
when we get off our high horses
and walk in understanding with other people.

You can once your mind is set to love
and you share peace with others wherever you go.

SEARCHING FOR A NEW HOME

I left Asia to seek out a new lifestyle
on the shores of Uncle Sam,
hoping the new land would be welcoming.
But I feared eyes staring at me everywhere I turned,
and for the first few times, it felt more real
than the lines on my palms.

I feared when I turned here or there,
there would be prickly gazes behind me,
or when I sat and smiled,
there would be quizzical stares that mocked me,
or every time I turned in my work,
there would always be some complaints here and there
to make me lose my calm.

But when I introduced myself to a few people
who were not from the same place I was,
they smiled, took my hand in theirs
and wrapped their arms around my shoulders.
"It's good to see your face.
You're welcome here," they said.
My confidence surged high,
knowing wherever I go, I would be welcome.

WAIT FOR YOUR TURN

Wait,
>Every day has a reward,
>Every move has a purpose,
>Every action has a reason and a consequence,
>Every question should have an answer,
>So why should I wait?

Wait,
>Every man has a purpose,
>Everyone wants a chance,
>Every child deserves to be loved,
>Everyone has a dream,
>So why should they wait?

Wait,
>Everyone wants a family,
>Everyone wants a home,
>Everyone needs a shelter,
>Everyone wants a better life,
>So why should they wait?

It is hard to wait.
Especially when you have a lot to share,
Especially when you have a dream,
Especially when a part of the world is waiting for you,
But your color holds you captive
In a foreign man's land
For a while.

You are told to wait for your turn
When it is already *your turn.*
The wait prolongs dreams
But cannot stop them.
Wait, just a little more.

WHOM TO FOLLOW

There are so many people in one place,
and the meeting is for one purpose.
The table brings all together as one,
but the chairs separate one from all.
Arguments reach the roof
as we rob and rub minds to reach a compromise.

Everyone has something to say.
Everyone believes his or her idea is best.
No one wants to hear from the other,
and yet we all want to work together.

We are raised by different hands
and in different homes.
Our beliefs differ,
and our values are each special.

We want what is best,
but do feel an only individual idea is better than the rest.
This is a huge task,
bringing forth various homes to make a home.
A decision must be made soon and fast,
but will we be able to put our differences to rest?
Even if it is just for a while,
we can reach our goals if we work as one,
even if we are leaves from different trees.

A BRIGHTER FUTURE

I speak to no one,
but I speak to someone,
who has toured some nations
and is tired of the same notions.
A little difference sets them apart,
but their actions are the same at heart.
One man believes we should move with time,
but another prefers we remain in the comfort of our kind.
Children travel far from their homes
to experience a new world,
but their expectations dwindle
as they are met with the trials of these new worlds.
Some turn back because they are unable to cope.
Others stay to surge ahead with little hope.
Slowly, they become a new man in a new home.
They struggle to learn all they need to about this home
as they face each day with a goal
in their unchanging heart.
At times they are robbed
of their rightful share of that earth and its hearth,
but they wear it on their hands
so that the future will be bright for them
as they play their part.

WHISPERS

Every turn I take, there is a voice.
Other times, there is more than one.
And in the darkest nights on those lonely streets,
I can still be seen by some who don't want me.

I am no creator but a creation;
Different but the same as the others.
They say it is not the same
Because the difference is clear in all I do.

I fight the urge to suppress the ache I feel
Just because I want to belong here:
A place where I am not wanted,
But a place I desire to be, where I seek to be accepted.

The days are longer,
And I have nowhere else to go.
Someday, I may be welcomed,
Even by those who close their hearts to me.

The whispers are sent to taunt me
Because I can tell what they are about,
But I will live like a deaf human,
One who doesn't have to endure cruel whispers.
Until then, I will walk in pride of who I am,
With the hope that someday,
We will live in love and acceptance.

GO OR EMBRACE ME

My hands are filled with choices.
The pair of compasses point at a direction,
but I am not ready to follow.
I do not want to set my feet upon new waters.

Every move I make,
The compasses keeps pointing to a particular point.
I have tried to turn a blind eye,
but I doubt I can ignore it for so long.

Should I return home or embrace this new air?
It may not hurt to give it a try,
but I don't want to forget my home.
I am scared of the move to make.

One part of me wants to flow with the air
because I am tired of being shut out.
Yet, another part wants me to stay back.

Both ways have their reasons,
but I am dangling on a thin rope,
one which may not hold me for long.

A decision must be made now.
I stare at my compasses
and move toward the direction.
I will embrace this new path,
for there is a deep peace I feel within.

HEROES OF ADVERSITY

A hero is an ordinary individual who finds the strength to persevere and endure in spite of overwhelming obstacles.

—Christopher Reeve

ENSLAVED NOT SHACKLED

Slavery is for the body; not for the mind.
Those were the strange words and a uniformed belief
that governed a certain Frederick Douglass's life.

He was born a slave and grew up as one.
All he knew was violence; he ate and drank it.
His life didn't get any better
when his parents' marriage hit the wall.

But he believed to be a slave shouldn't stop a human
from being regarded as a being who had rights,
like their masters and owners.

Like many slaves before him,
Frederick suffered at the hands of his cruel owners.
But he never succumbed
to the cruelty they visited upon him.
He ensured his soul remained
quite intact to function on its own.

He always knew life flowed through the pages of books.
He devoured as many books as he could find,
teaching himself until he was bold enough
to raise his voice and confront the oppressor.

With his convincing voice, he won many over to his side.
And both colored and whites soon joined his fight
in his quest to free all slaves
from the whip of their masters.

THE UNDAUNTED WOMAN

She knew poverty, like a friend that woke,
and slept, and dined with her daily.
While she grew, for her,
love was like the unreachable gold
in the deepest of mines,
not even from those
she held close to her and called family.

When a rapist came to her door,
when she was aged nine,
she sobbed and took the pain,
but fought the stigma with all she had.

And when at a tender age,
she felt her belly bear the pulse of another human,
she soldiered on, with all her might,
refusing to *kill* the fetus.
And when she had to watch the same child die in infancy,
she never gave up hope on herself.

"I will fight for myself and my life," she said,
and marched on to commandeer one of the best shows
that the world knows today.

If rural and urban Mississippi ever loved a woman today,
she would be dripping with love,
for she lives on,
as an icon for many girls who have dreams;
for she thrives on,
as a legend for many dreamers that have an oomph.

Oprah, she is, the daughter of Winfrey.

THE SEED OF HOPE

Life is a rollercoaster, and it never tells us
When the clock will come to an end for anyone,
But when we find out, we often come face to face
With the fear of dying, of leaving too soon,
Without having enjoyed life's fruits to the fullest,
And we crumble even before death comes.

But when life mocked Kris Carr
With a diagnosis of a rare Stage IV cancer,
It dawned on her that she had to treat her life
Better than she did before.
She buckled down and attacked cancer, head-on,
Refusing to lie back and let it have its way.

She equipped herself with weapons in books,
Life-saving documentaries, and a change in nutrition;
She launched a personal website
To save the lives of others.

And a decade later, she thrived healthily with cancer,
Carrying many others along on her journey
As an expert in the fight against cancerous diseases.

Today, many live healthily and peacefully
With the deadly disease
All thanks to her efforts to battle cancer herself.

BOUNCING BACK

How would you feel if, at a young age,
you made your first million dollars?

You would feel on top of the world, of course.
Imagine if you then had a change in fortune,
and you lost the same million dollars
at that same young age.

How would you feel then?
That gutted feeling in your throat
that nearly makes your eyes pop out of their sockets
is how Simon Cowell must have felt, if not worse.

Many people must have written him off
after losing his record company,
but he doubled back and found his path and calling again.
And today, he has become one of the biggest forces
on many reality TV shows.

Today, he is a judge that seals the fates of many,
because he understands that when you fall off your horse
and get hurt, you should never stay down.

Instead, rise to your feet, climb again
and continue until you finish your race,
because you never know if the last lap
will be your best yet.

THE ALL-SEEING EYE

No disability should give a human an excuse to give up.
No human with a *problem*
should ever bring themselves to stop,
for every human should strive for greatness;
chase it until their last breath departs their body
and they lose their wits.

When E.O. Wilson went blind in one eye,
many thought he would succumb
to his loss of partial sight.
Many thought he would drink himself to death,
or worse, take his life through other means instead.

But he found meaning in the pages of books.
He knew they were the secrets of life and many proofs
that life had more meaning and made more sense
when one became a quester.

His works earned him many bestselling books,
and he became a major contributor in different fields.
He rose to win the Pulitzer Prize,
not once but twice,
and his fame and fortunes never ceased to rise.

THE CHILD WITH STUMPS

The first cry of a baby was heard,
telling the world another king had come.
His parents were filled with joy
as they waited to hold their newborn.

Taken aback by the twist of fate,
they stared at the limbless innocent form.
At first, they stopped,
then pulled him into their warmth,
promising him all the love in their hearts.

Nick Vujicic enjoyed his parents' love
and had a normal childhood,
but suicidal thoughts crossed his mind,
making him want to end his life.

He picked himself up and surged ahead,
doing all that he loved the most,
not waiting on anyone to move around,
rather learning how everyone moved with ease.

Now he has a family of his own
and has become an inspiration to many,
crushing their thought
that being limbless would deter them
from pursuing their many dreams.

He grew to know who he is
and he has made the best out of his situation.

THE SCENT OF SUCCESS

Success follows people everywhere,
But first, it pushes failures in their paths
To see how they will respond to their calamity.
        It seeks to know whether they will give up,
        Or whether they will rise up.

And that is the same story for Bill Gates.
When he set out to market his Traf-O-Data,
When he got market for the device,
It didn't work.
        And although thoughts of quitting
        Might have flowed into his mind for a while,
        He never once listened to the temptation.

Instead, he set out again with Paul Allen,
A couple of years later after their epic fail,
To patent Microsoft.

Today, people see Bill Gates
As a model of true success,
For when the going got tough for him,
He got tough and got going, too,
Until he did it and became a renowned innovator
Because he believed success seeks out
The minds of true victors,
        And it dines with them forever.

THE POWER OF RAMBO

Look at him stand, a living hulk who doesn't cower
in the face of threats or hindrances.
Look at him taunt his detractors,
the man with little speech,
yet lots of actions, the kind that endears everyone to him.

Did you know some parts of his face were paralyzed?
Now you do.

But he never let his disability hamper his progress.
He boldly wears a mean look on his snarling face,
the kind that makes defeats and doubts wet their pants
when Sylvester stares at them.

Did you know his speech is slightly slurred?
Now you do.

But he never gave up on himself!
For he went on to be one of the most convincing actors
to ever grace our screens.

John Rambo, the defender of the defenseless.
Like a stallion, Stallone galloped over tons of challenges,
until he perched on high, like a bird with a vantage point.

And today, aside the many awards
that adorn his golden shelves,
the steps of the Philadelphia Art Museum
will forever bear his name,
and the world will forever marvel at his fame.

A STRONG WILL

I know a certain Richard Branson
whom everyone he came across called a bad student
when he was of a young age.
Perhaps because he was a victim of dyslexia,
many thought they could deride him and get away with it.
"You can't do anything right with books," they jeered.
"Leave school for the brilliant," others mocked.

But he would not back down nor ever say no
to the push of his strong will,
even when his results showed he wasn't doing too well
in any test that he ever completed.
"I can do anything I set my mind to," he murmured,
and slowly, his words began to shape his destiny.

Not once did he ever complain about his frailty
nor showed any signs of weakness.
Instead, he channeled the aura of his personality,
turned his life and status around
and drove himself toward success
without looking back.

THE LAST LAUGH

Show me a human who knew rejection
like the back of his hand;
I will show you
a man whose name echoes
through the halls of Hollywood today.

Show me a man who failed
to secure an admission
into his favorite school;
I will give you a name:
Steven Speilberg, the prolific filmmaker.

When life decided
to teach him a lesson about rejection,
it hit him
like the weight of a whole house.
It crushed him harder
than the hit of an articulated vehicle.

The film school of his choice
denied him a placement,
not only once but twice,
but he kept his head high,
and his mind worked like a clock.
He kept his heart in place,
and he put his brain to work.

And years later,
when he and success
ate from the same bowl,
the same institution gave him
an honorary degree.
Barely twenty-four months later,
he earned himself
a place as a trustee
of the same university.

Today, with him,
we know education is important,

but it may be a little overrated
on many occasions
because, in the end,
it is not only what one learns
in the four walls of a classroom
that defines one's life;
one also has to learn
outside the school
so that one's dreams
can grow wings
and fly beyond limitations.

With him,
we know life may laugh
at you many times,
but you may have
the last and longest laugh
if you persevere
and make tougher decisions
when it counts.

With him,
we know if you feed your dreams
with meals of hope and diligence
and water the seeds
of your goals with patience,
you will succeed.

THE PRESIDENT IN WHEELS

Perhaps you've heard of a man
who was dwarfed by many of his height.

I knew of one.

He did die many years ago,
but he wore bravery on his chest,
like an irremovable insignia.

Perhaps you've heard of a man
who succumbed his mobility
to the whims of polio.

I heard of him many years ago.
I still do today.

Franklin Roosevelt was a man who sat in the Oval Office
to rule the greatest economy the world knows today;
he was *the* man who gave men with two feet orders,
the kind no one could ever defy.
And not even his lack of feet could stop his resolve
for he knew so long as he breathed,
he could live on his terms,
according to his dictates.

So, tell me: Will you allow your fears to chain you
when you can tower above them
even when you are on wheels?

NO FINISH LINE

She only knew what the world looks like
For a brief stint of nine years
Until a disease stole her sight from her.

With a thing for shadows and shapes,
She lived her life through the worst situations,
But she made a paradise for herself and others
From the crumbling blocks of hell.

She ran her races without her sight.
Many she won with gold medals to show.
A few she lost with bravery,
But she earned herself priceless respect,
And not even her frequent pains could stop her
Quest for more knowledge, as she journeyed
Through life with enviable records and degrees.

If eyes were golden tickets to heaven,
She has none.
But she has a tenacity
That will make angels worship her,
On Earth and in heaven.

Her kind is rare,
Not because she is blind,
But because she gives her all to set others right.
She gives what she has to provide others
With a better world
Even without their sight.
Marla Runyan sees a worthy cause and a strength,
Where others see hopelessness and disability.

STRENGTH FROM A SHARK'S BITE

Not many can live to tell the tale
of a gruesome encounter with the ruler of the deep.
I read that a shark's bite often instantly kills
or leaves one too maimed to survive beyond a few hours.

But Bethany Hamilton did,
almost with pride in her eyes.
She was the victim of a shark's bite,
one good, hard bite was all it took from the cruel fish,
and one arm was cleanly sawn off from her shoulders.
But she punched death in the jaw
and swam herself to shore, even as she nearly lost herself,
thanks to too much loss of blood.

She had known surfing all her life,
and that near-death experience at age thirteen
wasn't enough to get her off the waters
or scare her away from her passion.
Nothing but her determination and grit got her through,
and nothing will keep her down
since she tasted true victory.

THE BREAKER OF PROTOCOLS

Ragnhild Kaata,
A Norwegian by birth who broke protocols.
Her story gave melody to the depressed,
Lifting even the lost souls
Until they sang her praises from their heart,
For she was the hope they had been waiting on.

She could not see the beautiful daisies
Or smell their sweetness.
She could not listen to the Nightingale's melodies,
No matter how much she tried.
Left in a world of her own,
She guarded her heart jealously,
Giving no room to the trusting arms,
Since she had woven a web around herself.

A smiling hand sought hers,
Promising to teach her about her world.
She was rigid but finally relaxed
To learn from her friend.

She broke a protocol in Norway,
One never accomplished by a disabled human.
She received proper schooling
And learned to speak like every other person.
She didn't stop with teaching herself;
Instead, she continued to inspire
Others like her to do the impossible.
She was a model and an angel
For many who were special,
Like her.

THE SCIENCE OF TENACITY

He was born like any other man, with complete organs,
a functional brain and a chipper lifestyle to match.
But while he rummaged through the world,
scouring every nook and cranny
for all kinds of knowledge
that could advance humanity,
tragedy struck.

His Achilles heel came in the shadow of ALS,
and the experts gave him
only two and a half years to survive
before he'd meet his maker,
a shocking revelation that shook King to his core.
Slowly, he lost his sensory functions and had to rely upon
the near-perfect aid of a machine
to perform at his near-best.

Unlike many who may cower in the face of death,
Stephen braced himself with his quest for knowledge,
and made laudable discoveries in his work.
And until he took his last breath, he never quit.

Indeed, he inspired people to look at the stars
and never at their feet!

THE COLORED SINGER'S SAGA

Jay-Z, he called himself.
From a rough neighborhood in Brooklyn,
he wanted to make it big as a singer,
but even bigger as a magician with words, a rapper.

He wanted his name on everyone's lips
and his music to make every girl shake their hips.
But many turned him away when he started out
on his quest to make his way through life,
saddled with his voice, his swagger, and his lyrics.

No one wanted him on their record label.
No human wanted to side with him or his dream.
No promoter wanted to listen to him or his songs,
perhaps because of his color,
his rugged looks, or some unknown wrongs.

So, he went all out to start his own record label,
Roc-A-Fella records he called it,
and like the name, he rocked more than a fella,
for everyone wanted to relate to him,
as he rose to unimagined fame.
He continues to make waves for himself,
a model for one
and many other colored humans like him.

NEVER QUIT

A child will marvel when they see a bulb
And turn it on for the first time.
They will gaze upon its brightness
As it fills the room,
And a smile will fill their cheeks
As they wonder how a single human
Could have put light in a bulb.

I bet you and I once marveled like that,
Wondering how long it took Thomas Edison
To try and fail at making a light bulb
Before he finally got the spark right,
Before he finally created his beacon of light.

Many say he tried a thousand times.
Others claim he tried
A thousand and ten places.
But all that mattered was that he kept at it
Until he got it right.

If one way doesn't work, try others
Because, like him, perhaps,
You should know that you cannot fail.
You can only find a million ways to try again.

THE STRANGE BRILLIANT MAN

I know of a strange man
Whose speech organs failed to work
For his first three earthly years,
But it never stopped his desire.

I know this same man like the back of my palm.
Indeed, for him, many have written epistles
And sung Psalms,
For his worth towers above many today and forever.

Albert Einstein was mocked by many,
Even those he called his friends,
And others who failed to know the true him
Called him a dud in class.
If only they knew Albert would become better,
If only they knew he would go on
To question everything we thought
We knew about the world.

Today, his works live after him,
For no human has ever willed their brain to work as he did,
And today, we know he showed us
Determination is all we need,
And a strong will and self-belief to succeed.

WHEN COMEDY SAVES

A child came to earth
like many before him,
but nothing seemed spectacular
about his birth
because his father lost
his source of income
no sooner than Jim
could answer his own name.

That crisis plunged the family into chaos,
and even he feared
that the Grim Reaper
would come for his parents.

Young Jim loved his books
and wanted to become famous in life,
but he couldn't study much longer
because there were no funds.
His parents could barely keep
the family's ropes together,
so they had to leave their home
since they were out of money.

A van became their home,
and they were always on the move.
Young Jim was ready
to cater to himself.
Because he loved his family,
he did the same for them.
Since school couldn't come to the rescue,
he took up a janitor role
so he could make ends meet.

At 15, he was angry at life,
but he knew his situation was only temporary,
and he always took solace
in comedy when he was down.

Fate was on his side

when he landed himself
a break in 1979
and a bigger one in 1983.
He never looked back since.
Have you ever seen
the comedy series *In Living Color?*
Or did you see *The Mask* or *Liar, Liar?*
Or *The Cable Guy* or *Batman Forever?*

If you did,
you're one of the lucky ones
to see him on screen
because you must surely know
the man behind the hit movies;
he's the same man,
the same comedian,
Jim Carrey,
who has put smiles on the faces
of many people for decades.

He isn't done yet
for he continues to do so,
better than before.

IT LIES WITHIN

I am a writer with a different touch,
but I was told my work could not be used.
I knew I wrote my best,
but they thought my first book was too small for them.

A lot of times,
they said no to my ideas.
Thirty times,
my novel was rejected.
Many times,
a door was slammed in my face.
Many years,
I cried myself to sleep clutching my papers.

So, I trashed it and gave up on writing altogether
until Tabitha found the manuscript.
"Stephen King, darling, please finish this work,"
she said, with a convincing voice.

And I did because I knew she was an angel
and I wrote from within,
my pen connecting to the heart of many.
I never stopped writing
until my works resonated with all and sundry.
Now, I am a bestselling author of many works,
because, with the help of my woman,
I didn't take no for an answer.

EMPOWERMENT THROUGH ADVERSITY

Adversity does not build character, it reveals it.

—James Lane Allen

THE FRUITS OF ADVERSITY

Show me a great human who ever lived
And escaped the clutches of a challenge in life.

No one. There never will be one.

Show me a human who can boast
That he never walked on hot coals
On their path toward their destiny,
And I will make a liar of them.

Without adversities, no human will treasure their glories.
They will waste the talents they are given
And become wanton fools,
The kind that will be merry
On someone else's hard-earned wealth.

Obstacles are the necessary evil for a successful life.
You cannot drink without breaking through a mountain.
You cannot eat without tilling the soil.
You cannot achieve a goal without striving for it.

And if you can persevere without a grumble,
Happiness will surely await you at the end of your journey.

I AM POSSIBLE

I was told to take a backseat again.
It was the third time in a row because of my blindness.
Unrelenting, I smiled and sat in the corner,
calculating, strategizing and making adjustments.
I was the only blind man in the organization.
The competition was stiff and almost impossible.
But every time, I beat those who were better than I am
　　　because I am possible.

I was told that I'd need a separate bus every day
because my weight tripled that of an average human,
but I smiled and thanked them,
knowing I decide who I want to be and how I want to be
　　　because I am possible.

I was told no orphan would make it by themselves
unless they wore the cloak of pity.
I shook my head in disapproval,
knowing that was not who I wanted to be.
So, I burned the midnight oil every day
and thirsted for knowledge like I would for water
until I became the best anywhere
　　　because I am possible.

THE POWER OF RESILIENCE

I once knew grief like the skin on my body.
I once dined with sorrow
and drank from the cup of sadness.
My dad lost a battle with cancer,
and my mom lost her senses and will to live
when the doctor broke the news to her.

I once thought Jack would love me forever,
but he woke one day and told me he was done with us.
And days later, Jean and Janet, my dogs,
slumped and died without symptoms.

I cried my eyes out, for my heartache was immeasurable.
At the time, I thought I should give up.
I wanted to end it all without blinking,
but I felt nothing should break me.
I understood I had to make tough decisions,
so I picked myself up from the dirt and vowed
never to gaze into the mirror of my past.

Today, I enjoy the love of a new partner,
tons of people who call me 'my child,'
and I have a dozen dogs
that wag their tails to welcome me home.

A CIRCLE

My home is not like any other.
It is filled with laughter and joy.
We hold each other during good and bad times,
and we share regardless of the quantity we have.
These are our practices for as long as time itself.

We moved to a new place,
where all was different.
We thought it absurd,
forgetting for a moment that culture differs.

The longer we stayed, the more we saw
and learned they did theirs in the way they thought best.
The theme of our differences formed a circle,
one filled with several beliefs but still a point.

We have learned that family differs everywhere we go.
We have learned that everyone is protecting his circle.
We have learned the power in differences.
We have learned the beauty in unity.
We have learned the beat of various languages,
and we have thrived with them despite the adversity.

THE STRANGER IN ME

Tossed out on a cold night
Alone to face dangers with no one in sight.
My feet stopped for seconds to look
At the stranger in me,
But I buried my face in shame
Because I detested my look in the clear water.

God, why did you create me in this form?
I kicked the empty air in frustration,
Angrily waiting for answers from the heavens,
But the clouds only opened,
Sending light droplets to my unanswered question.

The rain washed me anew,
Adding a new glow to my skin
And sending the stranger in me running.
The end of the rain brought light to my dark world,
And I saw the world from a new perspective.

Yes, I was born with no hands.
Yes, I was deprived of some beautiful gathering.
Yet, I felt hope rise from within,
One that would help me glide through the darkness.

PROOF OF KNOWLEDGE

Her parents wanted her
to be the best she could be,
though they barely had scraps
to feed her and her siblings.
So, she took to the streets
with dreams in her mind
and goods to sell on her head,
believing a day would come
for her to prove herself.

Whenever she returned home,
she'd sneak to her friend's adobe
to study her books
and answer her quizzes.
She would read
until her eyes ached.
She would read
until the information
became a part of her,
and while she studied,
she would help her friend,
who encouraged her
to devour every kind of knowledge
that came her way.

One day,
she came across two teenagers.
One was wailing,
and the other
was lying on the floor, unconscious.
She ran toward them,
and from what she had read,
she knew she had to resuscitate
the insentient teenager.
After a few tries,
the child woke up coughing.

A crowd had gathered
to watch the young seller display
the fruits of knowledge, and soon,
news about her spread like wildfire.

Many recognized her tenacity
and her desire for knowledge;
they encouraged her
to sit for exams
to prove her mettle.
And when she passed
with flying colors,
they told her
they'd sponsor her to study
to the ends of the world
so long as she promised
to continue to save lives.

And she did give her word
that as long as she took a breath,
she would dedicate her life
and work to saving the lives of others,
with passion as long as she breathed.

THE FUNCTION OF GOOD WORDS

I hear words are like a beacon that drives us
toward a destination, whether good or bad.

I hear words motivate you and like a forklift,
they help you out of the murkiest of situations.
I hear they move you even when you're at your lowest.

I hear words could become a weapon
that can protect you from the troubles of the world
if you make a mantra from them and chant them,
like a nursery rhyme on a daily basis.

I hear words can break you or change you,
depending on what you make of them in every situation.
So, when affliction comes knocking on your door,
or adversity engages you in a staredown,
do not be fearful,
for it is there to convey you
toward a growth that you need.

And with the right words,
you will increase the levels of your resilience.

So, when you feel like backing out
of the door to your dreams
because a series of misfortunes block your way, do not.

Instead, close your eyes, find the best group of words,
and keep plodding on;
see no blockade,
pay regard to no fears,
and slowly, like a cloudy sky, your adversity will flee.

THE PARADOX OF LIFE

Who would have thought
That nobody could be somebody?

Who could have thought
That a Black man could be the leader of a white race?

Who could have thought
That a supposed dull child could become a doctor?

Who could have thought
That a blind woman could have a formal education?

Who could have thought
All races could learn together without restrictions?

Who could have thought
All races could share a seat on a public bus?

The world is slowly awakening
From the misty form that it had in its eyes.

The world is stretching its hands
And giving abode to people of all descents.
Change is a constant variable.

And if the world did witness these changes,
If a lot could change when people have doubts,
Then don't think the lights of your hopes
Won't shine someday.

AT YOUR FEET

You tell me to stay,
Yet you push me aside.

You rob me in broad daylight,
Yet you pat me like a friend.

You steal from me to make yourself beautiful,
Yet you pretend I do not exist.

You learned my language, but when I turn my back,
You speak in a hushed voice.

At your feet,
I have moved with the ways of humankind,
For they are prone to the dictates of what they see.

At your feet,
I have seen a new picture and approach to life,
Serving as my manual to the breeze of life.

At your feet,
I have become stronger and wiser.
I have become independent and intelligent.

At your feet,
You once looked down your nose to see me.
I hid there until I got my stance and direction.

Now, I am above your feet.
I have been fed and am now ready
To assist others out there.
Because now I have thick skin, and others need one, too.